ALSO BY SHAUNA NIEQUIST

Bittersweet

Bread and Wine

Cold Tangerines

Present Over Perfect

Savor

LEAVING BEHIND FRANTIC FOR A SIMPLER, MORE SOULFUL WAY OF LIVING

STUDY GUIDE

FIVE SESSIONS

SHAUNA NIEQUIST

WITH ASHLEY WIERSMA

ZONDERVAN

Present Over Perfect Study Guide
Copyright © 2016 by Shauna Niequist

This title is also available as a Zondervan ebook.

Requests for information should be addressed to:
Zondervan, 3900 *Sparks Dr. SE, Grand Rapids, Michigan 49546*

ISBN 978-0-310-81602-7

Author is represented by Christopher Ferebee, Attorney and Literary Agent, *www.christopherferebee.com.*

Cover design: *Curt Diepenhorst*
Cover photography: *Aaron Niequist*
Interior design: *Kait Lamphere*
Interior image of chair: *PhotoDisc*

First Printing September 2016 / Printed in the United States of America

Contents

A Note from Shauna

Think for a moment about the word *perfect*. For far too many years, that's all I did: I thought about perfect; I worked toward perfect; I held up "perfect" as my prized ideal. I wanted perfect holidays and perfect vacations, perfect dinner parties and perfect celebrations with friends. Professionally, I wanted a perfect track record as one who always got everything done. And so I strived for perfect, I sacrificed too much for perfect, I pushed and proved and hustled and competed and went as hard and as fast as I possibly could—all for the sake of perfect, all in the name of realizing my elusive *perfect* dream.

I did these things because something inside of me said, "If you let up or slow down, you will lose."

Lose what, exactly? I wasn't sure, but I had my suspicions.

What if I lose my Most Dependable title?

Future job opportunities?

Admiration and praise?

In the end, what I lost was my soul, which is the very worst thing to lose.

I missed out on the life God had given me to live—to steward—because I was too busy building a different life, a life that looked more... perfect.

Along the way, I picked a different word to live by, a word that brought me back to that divinely gifted life. The word is *present,* and present is something perfect will never be. "Present is living with your feet firmly grounded in reality, pale and uncertain as it may seem," I wrote on the heels of that wind-whipped season. "Present is choosing to believe that your own life is worth investing deeply in, instead of waiting for some rare miracle or fairy tale. Present means we understand that the here and now is sacred, sacramental, threaded through with divinity even in its plainness. Especially in its plainness." *Present,* I found—and am still finding—is rejecting all the *climbing up* and choosing to simply come down. To come down to the ground, and to God, to the soil, the vibrations of life. Present is settledness. Stillness. Rest. Present is no to chaos and yes to calm. It is a deep-seated sense of allrightness ... it is acceptance and contentment and ease.

And so, the book (and this curriculum). It was four years in the making, and it is my invitation to you, to leave behind perfection-seeking and embrace presence as a way of life. It's better here, I promise—free from illusions, inspiring and good.

How to Use This Guide

Welcome to the video-based curriculum for *Present Over Perfect*. As Shauna has already mentioned, her deep desire is for the same level of spiritual sanity and settledness that she has come to know after walking through four of the most challenging—and rewarding—years of her life to be yours, fully and completely. To that end, she has put together a five-session experience aimed at helping you untangle whatever knots are keeping you from living the beautiful, orderly, God-centered life you were created to live.

BEFORE YOU GET GOING

To get the most out of *Present Over Perfect*, in addition to this study guide gather the following goods prior to diving in:

- The *Present Over Perfect* five-session video
- A copy of Shauna's book, *Present Over Perfect: Leaving Behind*

Frantic for a Simpler, More Soulful Way of Living (Zondervan, 2016)

- Your favorite Bible (this guide looks to *The Message*, but any translation is fine)
- A pen, and extra paper or a journal, in case you need more space to log your thoughts

NOTES FOR THE JOURNEY AHEAD

Consider rallying a few friends, family members, or colleagues to walk through this experience with you. Certainly, you can work through the content on your own, but the best growth happens in community, and while sharing your burdens aloud in the presence of other living, breathing human beings can feel a little scary at first, the support and strength you'll feel as a result of sojourning with others who also are choosing candor will be worth it in the end.

Once you confirm who will be joining you for the journey, choose a time and date to kick things off, and also decide how frequently you will meet. This guide has been arranged according to five sessions; divide those across five weeks, if you wish, or another interval that makes sense for your group. Regarding facilitation, feel free to rotate leadership responsibilities, or else declare one member the point person for all five sessions. Facilitation cues appear in blue italic type at the beginning of each section. And speaking of sections, there are six to be aware of. Here they are, explained:

- This Session: An overview of the theme covered that session/week.
- First Thoughts: An opening icebreaker for group discussion.
- Video Notes: Space to capture memorable quotes from the video segment.
- Inviting Others In: Questions for your group to discuss and answer.
- Practicing Presence: A closing liturgy for your group to read and reflect on.
- Solo Work: Questions, exercises, and journal prompts for you to complete between sessions.

If Shauna's firsthand experience thus far declares anything, it is that despite the messes we have made in life, by God's grace, we can *remake* something wonderful. Let the new edition begin!

Pain Points

⌐

It wasn't so long ago that we ourselves were stupid and stubborn, dupes of sin, ordered every which way by our glands, going around with a chip on our shoulder, hated and hating back. But when God, our kind and loving Savior God, stepped in, he saved us from all that.

—Titus 3:3–5, *The Message*[1]

THIS SESSION

Have a group member read the following paragraphs aloud as a way to center everyone's thoughts on this session's topic.

We're all pushing for something, for the life we think we want. We strive and strain and orchestrate and negotiate, in hopes of stitching together

---

1. All Scriptures from *The Message*, unless otherwise noted.

an existence that satisfies, but in the end, all that forced movement, all that contrived exertion, leaves us writhing in pain, in agony, right inside the reality we ourselves created.

The pain shows up in addiction. Or in a string of failed relationships. It shows up in overeating, overdrinking, overspending, overfunctioning, over-*everything*. This is because that ideal life keeps eluding us, and so we keep pushing harder to pin it down, and when those efforts keep proving futile, we keep needing a way to soothe the ache. But it's an ache that can't be soothed from the outside-in; tending to such a throb is always an inside job.

"I loved my life, but I had become someone I didn't want to be around," Shauna Niequist wrote in *Present Over Perfect,* a reflection on the too-busy, too-much life she'd built. "I had become someone I didn't want to be," she said, a self-assessment that would sober any-one. But honest self-assessment was her only option, so high was the pain she'd endured for four straight years. It has been said that nobody changes unless the pain is great enough; if true, she was primed for great change.

Her experience offers an invitation to us: will we let our pain get to unreachable levels before we correct course and tend to our soul? Or, if the pain is already screaming, will we muster the courage to listen to it for once, and *change?*

Session 1 explores the inner battles we all face and emboldens us with the reminder that the selfish structures we've built can be rebuilt, the harmful systems we've shaped can be reshaped, and the fruitless deeds we've done can be redone. That is, if we're willing to change.

"The things I had started off wanting—this life of meaning and depth and connection—was starting to be a life marked more by exhaustion, and loneliness, and isolation." —*Shauna*

FIRST THOUGHTS

Take a few minutes for your group members to share responses to the following question:

When have you experienced a moment of clarity such as the one Shauna described, when you realized that the life you were living had to change, and that the change must happen not whenever you found time to get around to it, but *now*?

VIDEO NOTES

Play the video segment for session 1 and use the prompts below to log your thoughts and notes.

A moment of realization

Pigpen's swirl of dirt and dust

Souls, and the tending they need

The ways we try to outrun our fear of facing the truth

"There's no there there"

When the ER visit is nonnegotiable

INVITING OTHERS IN

Discuss as many of the following questions as time and group interest permit.

1. Which of Shauna's reflections, assessments, or ideas from this session's video content resonated most with you, and why?

2. What emotions were stirred in you as you listened to Shauna describe her before-and-after moment in that Dallas hotel room, when she was desperate for her heavy, messy, disordered lifestyle

to change, and for the load she was carrying to be lightened somehow?

3. If you had to name the Pigpen-esque swirl of dirt, dust, and disorder that tends to follow you around, what would you call it? Constant drama, maybe, or chronic busyness? The drive toward perfectionism, perhaps, or the need to control? Why is it easier to acknowledge and name other people's swirls of dirt than to admit the one above our own head?

4. Shauna's Pigpen swirl manifested itself in daily life in two primary ways: First, it caused her to believe that she—as a highly capable, highly responsible woman, wife, mother, colleague, and friend— really could be everything everyone needed and do everything her heart desired. She referred to this as *pride*. Second, the swirl of disorder caused her to believe that gobbling up all life had to offer would somehow satisfy her soul. This was, to put it another way, *gluttony*.

   How do you respond to Shauna's assertion that we all have a certain battle to fight, as it relates to our particular "besetting sins" such as pride and gluttony, selfishness or gossip or rage? (See the box on the next page for more examples from Galatians 5.)

Have you ever sensed such a battle raging in your life? If so, describe for your group the dynamics involved.

"The two sins at play here, I believe, are gluttony and pride—the desire to escape, and the desire to prove, respectively. I want to taste and experience absolutely everything, and I want to be perceived as wildly competent." —*Shauna*

"It is obvious what kind of life develops out of trying to get your own way all the time:

- repetitive, loveless, cheap sex;
- a stinking accumulation of mental and emotional garbage;
- frenzied and joyless grabs for happiness;
- trinket gods;
- magic-show religion;
- paranoid loneliness;
- cutthroat competition;
- all-consuming-yet-never-satisfied wants;
- a brutal temper;
- an impotence to love or be loved;
- divided homes and divided lives;
- small-minded and lopsided pursuits;
- the vicious habit of depersonalizing everyone into a rival;
- uncontrolled and uncontrollable addictions;
- ugly parodies of community."

—*Galatians 5:19–21*

5. When we realize that the life we have created for ourselves is a far cry from the life we dream of, the gap between the two, as depicted below, can cause us to despair. How will we ever get from here to there? How can we close the gap?

These questions can seem unanswerable, and in our frustration and a deep-seated sense of futility, we turn to buffers such as busyness, overworking, striving and straining, working out obsessively, shopping compulsively, using harmful drugs, overindulging in alcohol, engaging in illicit sex, blowing money on gambling, and more—all in an attempt to build that coveted bridge.

How have you seen this dynamic play out in your life? What did you hope your preferred buffers would provide for you, and how well were they able to deliver on the promises they made?

6. In the end, none of those buffers can sustain us, and so we tumble even farther into the chasm we were trying to bridge. Have a member of your group read aloud Romans 7:14–20. Describe a time in your life when, like the apostle Paul, you have done the very things you hadn't wanted to do, only to discover that, as Shauna's friend Glennon[2] says, "there is no there there."

"The design flaw in all of it is thinking, 'If I do this, then I'll get this.' It's a faulty mechanism, all the way through." —*Shauna*

2.   Glennon Doyle Melton writes about this idea in her book *Carry On, Warrior: The Power of Embracing Your Messy, Beautiful Life* (New York: Scribner, 2013).

PRACTICING PRESENCE

Have a group member read aloud the liturgy below, and then take turns responding to the question that follows.

In this world, there will be challenge. There will be difficulty, and there
will be pain.

We ought to know. We have been filled to overflowing with those things.

This pain has looked like stuffing ourselves with experiences, with food,
with fake intimacy, with stuff.

This pain has felt like a weight around our necks.

This pain? It has sounded like screaming, like desperation, like
let-me-out.

It has smelled of fear.

It has tasted of regret.

This pain has left me hopeless, and yet isn't there always hope?

To be alive is to believe that hope beats alive still too.

My pain has been mine for so long, but it doesn't have to live
here forever.

There is a life I crave, a pain-free, rage-free life.

There, I can connect in meaningful ways with people . . . living,
breathing, blood-coursing-through-their-veins people. Imagine!

There, I can finally rest.

I can be enough there.

God *is* enough there.

If I work, I stay here. I get nothing.

But if God works, I go to the only there that *really is there*—the "there"
  of life that is truly life.
I wonder, Will I let him work in me?
Will I let myself go there?

Do you relate more to the "pain of here" portion of this liturgy, or to that which describes the "promise of there," and why?

"I had no idea how to get from here to there. But I knew that no matter what it cost me, I was going to find a way of living that was not marked by pushing, proving, earning, and competing." —*Shauna*

Pain Points

SOLO WORK

~

Work through this section on your own, before you gather with your group for session 2.

Of course, it is easier to keep buffering ourselves from the pain we feel than it is to address that pain head-on, to sit with it, to examine it, to understand it, to see it with soberness and clarity for what it is. But if we want change—real, lasting, useful, healthful change—then we will muster the courage and bravery it takes to raise our hand and say, "I'm in. Show me the burden I've been trying to carry in all its agonizing glory, so that *finally,* I can lay it down."

The following three sections are designed to walk you through the process of assessing the breadth and depth and weight of your present pain, the pain associated with living anything less than a life marked by complete peace, sturdy faith, assured value, authentic connection, and real rest. Work through them at your own pace, taking as much time with each as you need.

"The more I listen to myself, my body, my feelings, and the less I listen to the 'should' and 'must' and 'to-do' voices, the more I realize my body and spirit have been whispering all along, but I couldn't hear them over the chaos and noise of the life I'd created. I was addicted to this chaos, but like any addiction, it was damaging to me." —*Shauna*

REVIEW

Look back at the besetting sin you named in question 4 (pages 18–19) and jot it down again here:

Now, if you were to put words to that besetting sin, how would you define or describe it? What is it, and what is it not? How would a person know if she were struggling with it too, for example? Write out your thoughts below:

In your own life, how does this particular struggle hamstring you from living the way you desire to live? For Shauna, an example of *pride* included wearing herself out to the point of sheer exhaustion, for the sake of preserving the reputation of being a super-capable person. Furthermore, as she wrote in *Present Over Perfect,* her health and over-all well-being were crumbling:

> My health was suffering. I was frequently sick. I slept poorly and not enough. I got migraines and then vertigo. The muscles in my neck and shoulders felt more like rock than tissue, and the circles under my eyes looked like bruises. My heart—the heart I used to offer so freely, the heart I used to wear proudly on my sleeve—had retreated deep inside my chest, wounded and seeking protection. My ability to taste and connect and feel deeply had been badly compromised. My faith was stilted—it had become over time yet another way to try and fail, rather than a respite or healing relationship. (page 16)

What are the telltale signs that *you're* being negatively impacted by sin? Below and on the next page, give as many concrete, practical examples as you can think of. If it helps you to order your thoughts, simply finish the prompt provided for each example you list.

"One illustration of how this besetting sin has compromised my ability to be present, to enjoy life, to live simply, to thrive is . . ."

Example 1:

Example 2:

Example 3:

Example 4:

Example 5:

Example 6:

Example 7:

These examples you've acknowledged most likely converge to form a picture of the life you're working to escape from, the life on the left side of this chasm we looked at earlier:

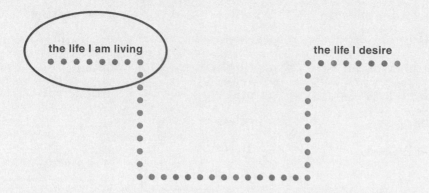

We'll look at the right-hand side of the chasm—the life you desire—in a future session, but for now, how else would you describe the life you're living now, the one that may need an overhaul, a rebuilding, right from the ground up? Circle any of the adjectives below and on page 30 that apply to the characteristics you'd like to leave behind, adding to the list on the blanks provided, if you wish.

burdened	anxious	joyless
competitive	tough	cutthroat
myopic/	fearful	lonely
hyper-focused	restless	loveless
heavy	regretful	isolated
efficient	exhausted	stuffed
effective	hard	divided
perfect	proud	hurried
sad	single-minded	brutal
busy	task-oriented	materialistic
stressful	frenzied	undisciplined

overdisciplined	reactive	exasperating
impersonal	unchecked	frustrating
addictive	compulsive	flabby
friendless	erratic	productive
harried	hopeless	_____
ugly	scattered	_____
selfish	snippy	_____
hustling	disheveled	_____
multitasking	structured	_____
rage-filled	wearying	_____

If you were to distill your current life into one sentence, how would you articulate your present reality? What is most true about you, today? Put down your thoughts in the space below.

Before you rush to the next part, sit with what you've written for a few minutes. I know, I know: you don't have time to do that. Such is the curse of the overbusy. Still, here is your chance, your opportunity to look squarely in the face of the truth about you—how you're doing, who you've become, what is real—and see it for what it is. It's the truth, but only for today. Our truth changes as we change: Remember, this is only session 1!

And so, we're back to the sitting-with-truth. Review everything from this Solo Work section that appears in your handwriting. See the words. Absorb the words. Let the realities they reflect hit you afresh. Turn on music, if you wish. Set a timer, if you must. But sit still. With your honesty, this honest look at your life.

In the blank space below, capture how you're feeling as you examine the pain you've endured—the pain you're perhaps enduring still. Draw a picture, pen a single word, print and paste a photo, sketch an emotion, copy a line from a song or a book, whatever. The goal here is intention, not perfection. Purposefully reflect what the pain elicits from you, as a way to mark this stage in your progress.

RECEIVE

It is normal to look at our specific besetting sins and determine that they are heavier or more consequential than anyone else's setbacks and struggles. This makes sense; we tend to be harder on ourselves than we are on other people. But God doesn't seem to support this type of assessment. Sin separates us from him, regardless of what kind of sin it is, and what seems of utmost importance to God is not parsing the nature of our deviation as much as the distance that deviation creates. He wants us close! As long as we're clinging to our sin—and to the buffers we inevitably employ, in hopes of numbing the pain we experience as a result of it—our hands aren't free to hold on to him.

Read the following two passages of Scripture for proof that God is not looking for us to clean up our act before coming to him. He doesn't care how we come; he just cares that we do. The first one is from Romans 5:6–8:

> Christ arrives right on time to make this happen. He didn't, and doesn't, wait for us to get ready. He presented himself for this sacrificial death when we were far too weak and rebellious to do anything to get ourselves ready. And even if we hadn't been so weak, we wouldn't have known what to do anyway. We can understand someone dying for a person worth dying for, and we can understand how someone good and noble could inspire us to selfless sacrifice. But God put his love on the line for us by offering his Son in sacrificial death while we were of no use whatever to him.

And then there is this one, from Titus 3:3–8:

It wasn't so long ago that we ourselves were stupid and stubborn, dupes of sin, ordered every which way by our glands, going around with a chip on our shoulder, hated and hating back. But when God, our kind and loving Savior God, stepped in, he saved us from all that. It was all his doing; we had nothing to do with it. He gave us a good bath, and we came out of it new people, washed inside and out by the Holy Spirit. Our Savior Jesus poured out new life so generously. God's gift has restored our relationship with him and given us back our lives. And there's more life to come—an eternity of life! You can count on this.

On the lines below, note a few findings from these Bible entries. Even if you've read these verses dozens of times, which words and phrases stand out to you this time around?

From the phrases you wrote above, put a check beside the one that feels most profound, relevant, or helpful to you here and now, based on how things are going today. Now, turn that entry into the backbone of a prayer or confession by completing the sentences below.

Dear God,

Thank you for your Word, which is alive and active and sharper than a two-edged sword. Thank you for the wisdom it offers me for daily living, and for the power it has to help me see with fresh perspective insights that can keep me from stumbling along life's path. As I read these two passages, I am reminded that . . .

_____

_____

What this tells me about you is that . . .

_____

_____

As it relates to my struggle—my "besetting sin"—what this means for me is that . . .

_____

_____

Please give me . . .

_____

_____

as I walk through this process of peeling back the assumptions, expectations, experiences, relationships, attitudes, motivations, and habits that have led me to where I am today.

Knowing that the swirl of dirt over my head doesn't disqualify me from intimacy with you makes me feel . . .

_____

_____

and realizing that in your presence, I can get back my life—real life,
abundant life, the life I was created for all along—makes me feel . . .

_____

_____

In a season of life when things can feel shaky, chaotic, and stuffed
full, I receive your words as blessing, as shelter in a time of storm.

**"I offer you the same encouragement my mentor gave to me: Stop.
Right now. Remake your life from the inside-out."** —*Shauna*

REMAKE

The rebuilding, the remaking, of a life doesn't happen in a quick,
sweeping stroke of a magic wand that can instantaneously transform
unrelenting freneticism into sanity, simplicity, and peace. No, more the
case it happens by way of baby steps—and not always forward-moving
ones, at that. "It can feel like two steps forward, three steps back,"
Shauna reminds us, which is admittedly a seemingly impossible way to
progress. The key here is that it's not always two-forward-three-back;
sometimes, you'll catch a stride.

Think back on your journey thus far. When have you seen small-step progress such as this firsthand? Maybe you picked up a new sport, or tried to learn how to play a musical instrument. You might have given a new language such as Spanish or Italian a try, or else perhaps you accepted a new role at work. Whatever the circumstances, there was a learning curve involved, and progress felt sluggish at best.

Describe the situation in the space below.

As it relates to reclaiming a sense of stability and beauty in your life, how willing are you to let progress be slow? To that end, consider incorporating the following handful of baby steps into your day today, and over the coming week. Read them over, give them a try, and dare to see what unfolds.

Baby Steps toward a More Soulful Way of Life

- **Catch your breath.** (Literally.) Take a deep breath—in through your nose for a slow-count of four; out through your mouth for eight. If you're feeling really ambitious, take *ten* breaths. Intentional breath-work is the sturdy base for a whole and healthy life.
- **Speak your besetting sin.** Say the words aloud: "I'm battling pride," for example. Or, "I tend toward gluttony." Or, "Some

days, anger consumes me." Bringing the struggling into the light immediately disempowers and defangs it; everything's scarier in the dark. Shine the bright beam of awareness by telling the truth, if only to God and yourself.

- **Keep the truth about you top-of-mind.** Remember: While you may be eager to take steps toward soulfulness, peacefulness, and a life that is marked by joy, your value as a human being is not contingent upon those changes being made. You are valuable here and now, today, with that dirt still swirling above your head. You were made on purpose, for a purpose. *You are already enough.*

A lined page follows, in case you want to log additional thoughts, observations, questions, ideas, or reminders, prior to your group convening for session 2.

Notes

The Roles We Play

⌒

Be energetic in your life of salvation. . . . That energy is God's
energy, an energy deep within you, God himself willing
and working at what will give him the most pleasure.

—Philippians 2:13

THIS SESSION

Have a group member read the following paragraphs aloud as a way to
center everyone's thoughts on this session's topic.

The natural question to ask, upon detecting pain in our lives, is, "Why do I hurt?" On plenty of occasions, we do this so reflexively that it barely registers as an intentional act. We wake up with sore hamstrings and in a flash think back on the grueling spin class we took the day before. We nurse a throbbing headache one evening while recalling that we totally forgot to drink water all day long. We stub a pinky toe and silently curse the ill-placed corner in the house that has nearly amputated that same toe a hundred times before.

But these are all examples from the physical world; is the cause of emotional, spiritual, or psychological pain as straightforward to detect? "As I peeled back the next layer," Shauna wrote, "I began to ask: why am I doing this? What is it in me that keeps things moving so breakneck fast, that believes achieving will keep me safe, that sacrifices my own health and happiness so that people who aren't me will think I'm doing a good job, in some vague, moving-target kind of way?" (*Present Over Perfect*, page 58).

In answer to her questions—questions that centered on that fundamental probe, "Why do I hurt?"—she would find staring at her a bevy of beleaguering roles, scripts that she had been handed months and years before, narratives that had surreptitiously dictated her decisions, actions, reactions, a whole *massive chunk* of her existence, for far too long.

Learning prewritten lines can be a fun thing to do if you're dabbling in drama or aspiring to the acting trade, but when it's real life we're talking about, the enjoyment fades. To have your steps marked out and your scenes blocked for you is to outsource your soul's care to someone else. And nobody can possibly manage another's inner world. These roles always do us in.

In session 2, we will look at the roles you may have been handed along the way, the effect they have had on your life, and what will be required of you in order to craft a new narrative now.

"I found myself playing this role: I was dependable. I was responsible. I was the get-it-done person. But I was exhausting myself. I was achieving, but I wasn't connecting. Something had to give." —*Shauna*

FIRST THOUGHTS

Take a few minutes for your group members to share responses to the following question:

Name a fictional television or movie character who (at least in part) reminds you of yourself, and explain why.

VIDEO NOTES

Play the video segment for session 2 and use the prompts below to log your thoughts and notes.

The roles we are given to play

Unlearning unhelpful patterns

Intensity in all of life

Doing for, instead of being with, loved ones

Working for, instead of lingering with, God

On writing a new script for life

INVITING OTHERS IN

Discuss as many of the following questions as time and group interest permit.

1. During the video's intro, when the women spoke of having been "slid" into various roles by other people, what thoughts or firsthand experiences came to mind? How well do you resonate with that idea?

"As I unravel the things that brought me to this crisis point, one is my own belief that hard work can solve anything, that pushing through is always the right thing, that rest and slowness are for weak people, not for high-capacity people like me. But at some point, good clean work became something else: an impossible standard to meet, a frantic way of living, a practice of ignoring my body and my spirit in order to prove myself as the hardest of hard workers." —*Shauna*

2. What role would you say you play—in your family of origin, in relationship to your spouse and children, at work or school, in your circle of friends, and so forth? If you were asked to assign descriptors to it, what words would you use? Some examples follow, to help wrap your mind around the idea. Circle any that may apply to you, place a star beside the one that *most* reflects your life, and then discuss your selections with your group.

The dependable one	The workhorse	The cynic
The shock absorber	The pessimist	The naysayer
The cautious one	The decision maker	The spontaneous one
The caregiver	The boss	The life of the party
The relational glue	The ideas person	The pusher
The social planner	The control freak	The negotiator
The people pleaser	The available one	The multitasker

The funny one	The jokester	The others-centered
The loving one	The beauty	one
The topper	The sports buff	The best mom
The skeptic	The trivia hound	The eternal
The know-it-all	The creative one	optimist
The talker	The health nut	The inexhaustible
The holy one	The equivocator	one
The deep one	The one in the know	The self-deprecating
The encouraging	The peacemaker	one
one	The giver	The one who has it
The quiet type	The questioner	all together

3. For most people, there is a definite upside to playing the role they have been given to play. They receive praise for playing that role, perhaps, or are found attractive or competent in some regard for playing that role. They are handed interesting opportunities or are included in highly desirable circles. They are invited into the game—whichever game it is that they want to be playing.

   As you consider your current role in your various spheres of influence, what benefits might you be receiving from agreeing to play it?

4. Now, to the flip side of the coin. Shauna talked in this session's video segment about the fact that playing the role of the ultra-dependable, get-it-done workhorse caused her to begin prizing efficiency in key relationships more than genuine connection, among other negative effects. What sacrifices do you find yourself making in order to play the role you find yourself playing?

5. Read the story of Abraham, Sarah, and Abimelech found in Genesis 20:1–18. What fears kept Abraham from asking Sarah to play a role she never should have played? Surveying the landscape of your own heart, what fears or concerns do you have about letting go of the role you're known for, even if the cons of playing it clearly outweigh the pros?

6. The characteristic Shauna said she lost along the way—to her tragic liability of insisting on playing her workhorse role—was that of whimsy. If you could reclaim one trait, one thing that used to be true of you but that you dropped along the way, what would it be, and why? Choose a word from those at the top of the next page, or come up with one of your own to share with your group.

generous

TEACHABLE   childlike

UNSTRUCTURED   spontaneous

outgoing   optimistic   ENGAGED

buoyant   silly   joyful   spiritual

happy   ENERGETIC   OTHERS-CENTERED

nonjudgmental

disciplined   kind   LOVING

connected   present

whimsical

"Those skills I developed that supposedly served me well didn't actually serve me at all. Inch by inch, year by year, they moved me further and further from the warm, whimsical person I used to be. And I missed her." —*Shauna*

PRACTICING PRESENCE

Have a group member read aloud the liturgy below, and then take turns responding to the question that follows.

I was handed this script, the script whose lines had me playing this
character, this role.

I'm the workhorse. The optimist. The giver. The life of the party.

Where did it come from? Who did the handing?

Parents, certainly. Siblings. Teachers. Coaches. Encouragers and
critics and friends.

These roles get honed at home and at church, at school and at work . . .

Everywhere, everyone confirms "my role."

My role is so helpful, so useful, so important . . . for *them.*

But for me? If I'm not careful, that helpful, useful role I'm playing will
suck the health right out of my soul.

The roles themselves? They're neither good nor bad.

They just *are*—they are what they are.

It's when I look to my role for my value that I get myself in trouble.

For so long, I've done just that, to the point that I wonder who I am
apart from the role I play.

If you're always dependable, when can you ever let something slide?

If you're always funny, when can you have a serious thought?

If you always have it all together, when can you call a friend and weep?

I've settled on the answer, "Never." Or that's what my actions
say, anyway.

Those actions say, "Obviously, this role is far too important for me to lay

it down. Who in his or her right mind would lay it down?"

And yet look at all this pain it's causing, the thousand ways it wrings

me dry.

Maybe it's time for a new narrative . . . one that, together, God and I craft.

Maybe it's time to be open to that.

What is it that your role never allows you to do? Let something slide?

Have a serious thought? Call a friend and weep? Something else?

The Roles We Play

SOLO WORK

~

Work through this section on your own, before you gather with your group for session 3.

The cosmic pain we're experiencing day by day is often caused by the fact that we're utterly unwilling to lay down the very roles that are exhausting and exasperating us. It's the equivalent of complaining of heat while grasping the grate of a fired-up grill; if only we'd release our grip, the searing pain would fade away.

And so it is with emotional and spiritual turmoil; as soon as we let go of the offending agent—in this case, someone else's idea of who we are, of the role we believe we must play—we experience the peace and freedom we were made to enjoy; in biblical terms, "abundant life."

Your Solo Work this time involves looking closely at the key role you've been holding on to, and mustering the resolve to release your grip.

"For so many years, I was deeply invested in people knowing that I was a very competent, capable, responsible person. I needed them to know that about me, because if that was true about me, I believed, I would be safe and happy. If I was responsible and hardworking, I would be safe and happy." —*Shauna*

REVIEW

Glance back at question 2 (page 44) from this session's "Inviting Others In" section and locate the role you starred, the one that most closely reflects how you've lived your life thus far. Write that role on the line below.

_____

Shauna referred to the origins of the role each one of us plays as a "complex soup" made with the ingredients of our upbringing, our church experiences, and the (often well-intentioned) messages we receive from family members, work colleagues, friends, and so forth.

Look back on the inputs you've received along the way. Within each of the following categories, think of a time when you were told how to behave or what to say, what to think or how to respond. In the space below each header, describe the experience and the meaning you drew from it. An example from Shauna has been provided.

Messaging from parents:

Example: *Even as a young child, each time I overcame a challenge, I was told that I was "tough" and "capable" and "strong." The adjectives became something of a self-fulfilling prophecy, in that the more I heard those words, the more I behaved in a tough/capable/strong way.*

Messaging from siblings:

Messaging from friends:

Messaging from church:

Messaging from teachers or coaches:

Messaging from bosses or colleagues:

Other messaging I received:

"Oh, the things I did to my body and my spirit in order to maintain my reputation as a high-capacity person. Oh, the moments I missed with people I love because I was so very committed to being known as the strongest of the strong. Oh, the quiet moments alone with God I sacrificed in order to cross a few things off the to-do list I worshiped." —*Shauna*

In the next part, we will explore how these various messages stack up against the messages God has imparted to us—about who we are, who he is, and where those two realities intersect.

RECEIVE

The Bible brims over with divine offers from a loving God to his people, provisions and promises he longs to fulfill in our lives, if only we will let him in. Take a look at some of these offers (below and on the next two pages), jotting down in the space provided your interpretation of each as you go.

"I will abide with you." (John 15:7)

"I will protect you." (Psalm 121:7)

"I will provide for you." (Romans 8:32)

"I will fight your battles." (Exodus 14:13–14)

"I will accomplish good things through you." (Philippians 2:13)

"I will remove your fear." (Matthew 6:25–34)

"I will carry your burdens." (Matthew 11:30)

"I will be a friend to you." (John 15:15)

"I will be your strong tower." (Psalm 46:1–6)

"I will never leave you nor forsake you." (Deuteronomy 31:6)

"I will lead you beside still waters." (Psalm 23:2)

"I will give you abundant life." (John 10:10)

"I will give you strength." (Isaiah 40:29)

"I will give you rest." (Matthew 11:28)

"I will collect your tears." (Psalm 56:8)

"I will perfect you." (Philippians 1:6)

"I will guide you in righteousness." (John 16:13)

"I will give you peace." (John 14:27)

The list goes on and on, but the myriad entries all point to one simple truth: God wants to play *all the roles.* All the pushing and producing, all the straining and striving, all the contrivances and role-playing and hustle and bustle and forcing and finagling and drive—to *all* of it, God says, "Here. I'll take that—really. I never meant for you to carry that load."

"I have left behind some ways of living that I believed were necessary and right that I now know were toxic and damaging, among them pushing, proving, overworking, ignoring my body and my spirit, trusting my ability to hustle more than God's ability to heal." —*Shauna*

In the space that follows, reflect on why you sometimes rely on yourself— your own ingenuity, your own determination, your own tenacity, your own strength—more than on God's offers of sufficiency and grace. How did the messages you received along the way fuel your sense of independence? In what ways have your personal successes caused you to lean into your own capabilities instead of God's? What doubts or fears keep you from more fully trusting him?

REMAKE

In a coming session, we will look at how to get from the life we're living today to the more soulful, God-dependent way of living, as represented by the "life I desire" side of the graphic, below.

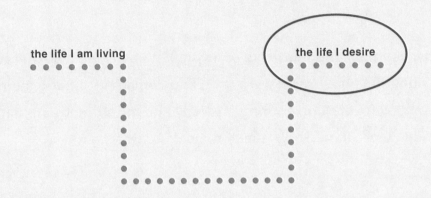

But for now, as a precursor to that discussion, take a few moments to think carefully about the key role you've been playing, and what you stand to gain by letting someone else play it awhile. That someone else? He is God. In your mind's eye, envision turning over that role to him—at least for a season—and allowing him to play the part you've been so frantically trying to play.

Picture yourself handing him the script—every line, every stage cue, every scene—and then picture yourself weightless and free. Ready for a baby step you can take right now, today? If you're the control freak, let things unfold unorchestrated, just for this day, this week. If you're the chronic overworker, pick up a magazine and plop down on the couch. If you're the relational glue in your family, forego the hyper-communicative phone calls just once. If you're the health nut, try a donut hole. Loosen your grip on the role you've been playing long enough to toy with allowing a new narrative in. You might be shocked to learn the world will keep spinning, and that you're a whole lot happier in the end.

Notes

Yes, and No

*I will praise the L*ORD*, who counsels me; even at night my*
*heart instructs me. I keep my eyes always on the L*ORD*.*
With him at my right hand, I will not be shaken.

—Psalm 16:7–8 NIV

THIS SESSION

Have a group member read the following paragraphs aloud as a way to
center everyone's thoughts on this session's topic.

In the last session, we looked at the messages we've received that influence the roles we wind up playing, and while it is true that those "other people"—family members, siblings, pastors, teachers, coaches, colleagues, and more—do help to shape the scripts we live from, we ourselves are culpable too. For starters, we accept the role. We persist in the role. If we receive enough affirmation for playing it, we even *perfect* the role over time. Despite our suspicions that the role may not be serving us well, we keep saying yes to playing it, in a thousand different ways, day by day.

"Yes! I'll host your baby shower. And *yours* . . . And yours too . . ."

"Yes! If the shirt is *that* price, I'll take the blue one and the striped one as well."

"Yes! I can watch your kids for you today. And tomorrow too? Sure thing."

"Yes! I can be there Thursday. And I can stay as long as you need."

"Yes! Pour me another. What's a party without a few glasses of wine?"

"Yes! I'd love to meet to talk" (even though as usual she'll be the only one talking).

"Yes! We'd love to vacation with you! We're crazy-busy that month, but we'll make it work."

"Yes! I can be the superstar contributor again this quarter, coming early and staying late."

"Yes! I can bring dinner to you tonight. Really! It's no trouble at all."

The common denominator here, of course, is "yes"—the word that strings together our burdens, one agreement at a time.

"Yes says possibility! It says adventure! It says life. But you can't have yes without no." —*Shauna*

For all its sparkly possibility, "yes" only tells half the story, because you can't have *yes* without *no*. Each time you offer a yes, you by definition also offer a no. Or a *series* of nos, depending on how consequential that yes proves to be. Take, for example, the "yes" you give to bringing dinner tonight to your sick friend and her whole family—that yes seems innocent enough, right? But that split-second decision means a last-minute trip to the grocery store, and then food prep in addition to the accommodations you were already making for your own family's meal, and then the drive to your friend's house, and then twenty or thirty minutes spent getting the complete health update while you lovingly drop off the food.

The time and energy spent fulfilling that one quick yes takes resources away from the people you love *even more than* your beloved friend. The simple *yes* you offered her just might equate to *no* for your family tonight.

"If you're not careful with your yeses, you start to say no to some very important things." —*Shauna*

To be sure, if this were a one-time occasion, all would be forgiven and nothing would be lost. But remember, we're talking here about *roles* we're playing, not one-off anomalies, exceptions to the rule. It's not that you agreed to bring this one meal; it's that you're *forever* bringing meals.

Your role is, "Meal? Okay! I'm in!" even as your better judgment hollers, "Nooooo!"

You learn of the need and you say *yes* to the need, serving up for your family (and your soul?) another *no*. It's just one of a million examples of how we choose the chaos we live.

In this session, we'll delve into the yeses and nos that dictate our actions, which then determine the pace of—and the peace in—our lives. So much of life comes down to two simple words—yes, and also no.

"I realized all at once that I'd spent all my yeses, and in order to find peace and health in my life, I needed to learn to say no." —*Shauna*

FIRST THOUGHTS

Take a few minutes for your group members to share responses to the following question:

When a seemingly great opportunity is in front of you, how do you decide whether to seize it or politely decline?

VIDEO NOTES

Play the video segment for session 3 and use the prompts below to log your thoughts and notes.

"What are you going to do?"

On deciding to put up more chairs

Loving yes

The dangers of yes

Saying no, to get back to yes

The ripple effect of a well-placed "no"

INVITING OTHERS IN

Discuss as many of the following questions as time and group interest permit.

1. Are you by nature more of a spontaneous/adventuresome/eager "yes" person or more of a well-ordered/circumspect/sober-minded "no" person? What predispositions, priorities, or experiences have shaped you in this regard?

2. Look over the themes and realities of your life today and assess how many "chairs" are currently set up. A "chair" for you could be volunteering at your child's school; or being the one your friends can call on whenever they need a hot meal, a ride, childcare, or a listening ear; or the worker who will stay late to make sure the project is completed; or serving at the church's missions festival again.

    How satisfied or dissatisfied are you with the number of chairs you see set up? What thoughts come to mind as you consider the fact that you can add or take down chairs at will?

"The idea that you could intentionally make something smaller or simpler felt surprising—and exciting—to me." *—Shauna*

3. Consider an aspect of your life where you desperately want to say no but have convinced yourself that your participation there is nonnegotiable—keeping your house well-ordered and clean, perhaps, or educating your children in a nontraditional manner; working full-time outside the home, serving in a particular capacity with your church, managing your family's finances, keeping a full social

calendar, shuttling your kids to various activities, or something else entirely.

If you were given permission to remove one such "chair" from your life, which would you remove, and why?

4. Read Jeremiah 2:4–19, which includes a harsh prophetic word for the nation Israel, a group of people who perfectly (and tragically) demonstrate what it looks like to have misplaced yeses and nos. In what ways is the chair you should have (but haven't yet) removed like the leaky cistern described in verse 13?

5. What positive changes in your life would you realize if you said no to this one leaky thing? How meaningful would those benefits be to you?

PRACTICING PRESENCE

Have a group member read aloud the liturgy below, and then take turns responding to the question that follows.

Yes.

And no.

Two game-changing, path-paving words.

Yes to this, no to that, and before you know it, the course is set,

The course marked by contentment and calm, or else by chaos

    and craving,

By pushing and hustling and stress.

"Come to me, you who are weary," God says.

"Come to me, and I'll give you rest."

I want that rest, but who has time?

My yeses have left me too busy.

Too busy being . . . busy.

Rest.

The word alone makes me ache.

I'm tired at a level that sleep on its own can't address.

I'm *soul-tired.*

Something is off in my soul.

The something comes down to yes, and also no.

Those yes-yes-yeses, they were rampant,

And consequential like you can't believe.

Those yeses I so quickly said made me say no, and no, and no.

No to things that matter,

No to family,

No to soul-care.

No to rest and groundedness,

No to connection and peace.

I don't want to be a "no" person! Life is too short for no.

And yet in this season, I see no for what it is:

An anchor, a life-preserver, a friend.

When have your yeses left you "soul-tired"? When have you wished for "no" to be your anchor, to be your friend?

"You don't have to damage your body and your soul and the people you love most in order to get done what you think you have to get done." —*Shauna*

SESSION 3

Yes, and No

SOLO WORK

Work through this section on your own, before you gather with your group for session 4.

There are circumstances, dynamics, and obstacles that for the moment, anyway, are beyond our control. Single moms know this. Those with chronic pain know this. Anyone working two jobs is all too aware of this truth. People with addicted family members; people suffering terrible disease; people whose credit cards got stolen last week; people who now face months and months of rehab, all because they slipped on the ice this past winter and fell—these people are keenly aware that there are some things you just can't change. But of course that's only half of the story, given the myriad things you *can.*

This section is about cataloguing those changeable things, in anticipation of perhaps doing that very thing—*changing them*—in the sessions to come.

71

REVIEW

In the video segment, Shauna alluded to the enticing nature of the word *yes*. Yes is full of possibility and promise, of excitement and adventure and fun, which is why it is all too easy, when assessing the yeses in our life, to hyper-focus on the wonderful, undeniable benefits they afford us, thereby downplaying those yeses' true cost. We do this with the roles we play, and also with the decisions that flow from those roles.

This brings us to two helpful questions:

- What are your yeses costing you?
- Is this a wise price for you to pay?

Flip back to find your answer to question 3 from this session's "Inviting Others In" section regarding the "chair" you wish you could remove from the room of your life. Note that involvement/obligation/commitment/endeavor on the line below, beside the chair icon. Then, answer the three questions that follow.

Assessing My Yes

_____

Write a description here of the "yes" you'd like to remove.

1. Every yes provides us some set of benefits; otherwise, we would never have said yes in the first place. For example, in saying yes to lots of work-related travel, a whole host of speaking engagements, and multiple simultaneous writing projects, Shauna netted for herself, among other benefits, the admiration of her extended family, her friends, and her publisher; an exciting, adventure-filled week-to-week reality; and a good paycheck.

   As you look at the yes you wrote, think about the things you've gained as a result of it. Jot down as many benefits as you can.

2. The benefits of our yeses represent only one side of the equation, for even the most wonderful opportunities always demand something in exchange. There is a cost attached to every yes, be it emotional, physical, financial, relational, spiritual, practical, or some combination thereof. Glance back at the yes you noted on the previous page. What has that yes cost you so far? What does it continue to cost you today? Log your thoughts below.

3. Looking at your answers to the two previous questions, and based not merely on the sheer quantity of them (how many entries there are), but also on the quality (how consequential each entry is), how would you assess this particular yes? Check one of the boxes below.

   ☐ In my gut, I'd say that the benefits of this yes outweigh the costs.

   ☐ I have a sinking feeling that the costs of this yes outweigh the benefits.

   ☐ The benefits and the costs of this yes feel pretty equal to me. I could go either way.

In session 4, you will be invited to further work through the assessment you just completed by asking God how *he* would weigh in. Does he see more benefit to you than cost? More cost than benefit? Overall, is this a yes he would have you maintain? It was only through soliciting divine input of this kind that Shauna was able to accurately determine the yeses she should keep and the ones she should release. Perhaps the same path will prove useful for you.

In advance of that exercise, you may wish to assess additional yeses in your life. If so, blank assessment pages appear at the end of this session, on pages 81–90. Once you have completed all of the assessments you wish to work through, move on to the "Receive" portion of the Solo Work.

RECEIVE

If this is the first time you have worked to honestly assess what your yeses are costing you, take heart: Even if the cost is higher than you would have guessed, the process of rightly calculating it is never in vain. Consider this word of encouragement, straight from the lips of Jesus:

> "Is there anyone here who, planning to build a new house, doesn't first sit down and figure the cost so you'll know if you can complete it? If you only get the foundation laid and then run out of money, you're going to look pretty foolish. Everyone passing by will poke fun at you: 'He started something he couldn't finish.'
>
> "Or can you imagine a king going into battle against another king without first deciding whether it is possible with his ten thousand troops to face the twenty thousand troops of the other? And if he decides he can't, won't he send an emissary and work out a truce?"
>
> —*Luke 14:28–32*

The encouragement is this: if the refusal to count the cost renders you and me a fool, then the willingness to count it declares us *wise*. And who doesn't want to be considered wise?

In the box on the next page, write a prayer to God asking for the courage and strength to examine with fresh perspective the yeses and nos in your life. Ask him to prepare your mind and heart for the direction he plans to give you in the final two sessions regarding remaking your life from the inside-out. Then, move on to the "Remake" section.

Dear God . . .

"'No' would become the word I would use, to reshape the edges and dimension of my life. As a person who wants to live so much 'yes,' this would prove very difficult for me." —*Shauna*

REMAKE

Let's look at one final aspect of the costs associated with the things you're saying yes to today—namely, the impact those yeses are having on the people you know and love. Our lives don't exist in a vacuum in which our decisions matter to us alone; our choices affect friends and family, and that cost must be calculated too.

Picture your relationships like concentric circles: the inner circle is your spouse if you are married, your children if you have them, your closest confidants, your very best friends.

The next circle out is your extended family and good friends.

Then comes the people you know, but not well—colleagues, and ministry partners, maybe. People you cross paths with often, even if they've never set foot in your home.

The circle way out on the edge of things is where acquaintances and friends-of-friends are. If you have a knack for interior design, for example, this is random Jane Doe sending an email to you one morning, to explain that she is Facebook friends with someone you know well and to ask if you could give her some tips on decorating her new home. You may feel a strange sense of obligation to fulfill the request out of deference to that mutual friend, but still, upon close inspection, Jane Doe is a fourth-circle connection and no more.

"What I've learned the hard way is you don't answer to a wide swath of people and their opinions, even if they're good people, with good opinions. You were made by hand with great love by the God of the universe, and he planted deep inside of you a set of loves and dreams and idiosyncrasies. You can ignore them as long as you want, but they will at some point start yelling. Worse than that, if you ignore them long enough, they will go silent, and that's the real tragedy." —*Shauna*

Take a look at the graphic below. Then, on the chart that follows, begin to map your current relational connections by noting your first-level, second-level, third-level, and fourth-level ties.

Relational Circles, Defined

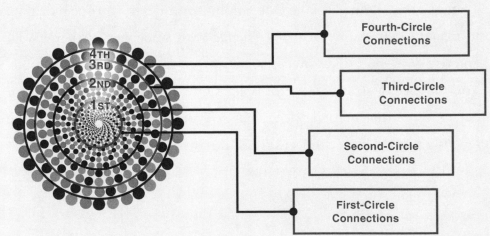

Charting My Relational Connections

First-Circle Connections	Second-Circle Connections	Third-Circle Connections	Fourth-Circle Connections
[God + closest confidants]	[extended family, good friends]	[people you know, but not well]	[acquaintances, friends of friends]

On pages 72–74, you made an honest assessment of the impact one of your key yeses is having on your life. Now, assess that yes in light of the relationships you most prize. On the graphic below, note in the blank boxes any first-circle, second-circle, third-circle, or fourth-circle connections that are being negatively impacted by this particular yes. Then, in the space that follows, capture any thoughts that come to mind regarding the nature of this impact, so that the information will be top-of-mind as you head into session 4.

Those Adversely Affected by My Yes

Assessing My Yes

Write a description here of the "yes" you'd like to remove.

1. Every yes provides us some set of benefits; otherwise, we would never have said yes in the first place. For example, in saying yes to lots of work-related travel, a whole host of speaking engagements, and multiple simultaneous writing projects, Shauna netted for herself, among other benefits, the admiration of her extended family, her friends, and her publisher; an exciting, adventure-filled week-to-week reality; and a good paycheck.

   As you look at the yes you wrote, think about the things you've gained as a result of it. Jot down as many benefits as you can.

2. The benefits of our yeses represent only one side of the equation, for even the most wonderful opportunities always demand something in exchange. There is a cost attached to every yes, be it emotional,

physical, financial, relational, spiritual, practical, or some combination thereof. Glance back at the yes you noted on the previous page. What has that yes cost you so far? What does it continue to cost you today? Log your thoughts below.

3. Looking at your answers to the two previous questions, and based not merely on the sheer quantity of them (how many entries there are), but also on the quality (how consequential each entry is), how would you assess this particular yes? Check one of the boxes below.

☐ In my gut, I'd say that the benefits of this yes outweigh the costs.

☐ I have a sinking feeling that the costs of this yes outweigh the benefits.

☐ The benefits and the costs of this yes feel pretty equal to me. I could go either way.

Assessing My Yes

Write a description here of the "yes" you'd like to remove.

1. Every yes provides us some set of benefits; otherwise, we would never have said yes in the first place. For example, in saying yes to lots of work-related travel, a whole host of speaking engagements, and multiple simultaneous writing projects, Shauna netted for herself, among other benefits, the admiration of her extended family, her friends, and her publisher; an exciting, adventure-filled week-to-week reality; and a good paycheck.

   As you look at the yes on the line above, think about the things you've gained as a result of it. Jot down as many benefits as you can.

2. The benefits of our yeses represent only one side of the equation, for even the most wonderful opportunities always demand something in exchange. There is a cost attached to every yes, be it emotional,

physical, financial, relational, spiritual, practical, or some combination thereof. Glance back at the yes you noted on the previous page. What has that yes cost you so far? What does it continue to cost you today? Log your thoughts below.

3. Looking at your answers to the two previous questions, and based not merely on the sheer quantity of them (how many entries there are), but also on the quality (how consequential each entry is), how would you assess this particular yes? Check one of the boxes below.

    ☐ In my gut, I'd say that the benefits of this yes outweigh the costs.

    ☐ I have a sinking feeling that the costs of this yes outweigh the benefits.

    ☐ The benefits and the costs of this yes feel pretty equal to me. I could go either way.

Assessing My Yes

Write a description here of the "yes" you'd like to remove.

1. Every yes provides us some set of benefits; otherwise, we would never have said yes in the first place. For example, in saying yes to lots of work-related travel, a whole host of speaking engagements, and multiple simultaneous writing projects, Shauna netted for herself, among other benefits, the admiration of her extended family, her friends, and her publisher; an exciting, adventure-filled week-to-week reality; and a good paycheck.

   As you look at the yes on the line above, think about the things you've gained as a result of it. Jot down as many benefits as you can.

2. The benefits of our yeses represent only one side of the equation, for even the most wonderful opportunities always demand something in exchange. There is a cost attached to every yes, be it emotional,

physical, financial, relational, spiritual, practical, or some combination thereof. Glance back at the yes you noted on the previous page. What has that yes cost you so far? What does it continue to cost you today? Log your thoughts below.

3. Looking at your answers to the two previous questions, and based not merely on the sheer quantity of them (how many entries there are), but also on the quality (how consequential each entry is), how would you assess this particular yes? Check one of the boxes below.

   ☐ In my gut, I'd say that the benefits of this yes outweigh the costs.

   ☐ I have a sinking feeling that the costs of this yes outweigh the benefits.

   ☐ The benefits and the costs of this yes feel pretty equal to me. I could go either way.

Assessing My Yes

Write a description here of the "yes" you'd like to remove.

1. Every yes provides us some set of benefits; otherwise, we would never have said yes in the first place. For example, in saying yes to lots of work-related travel, a whole host of speaking engagements, and multiple simultaneous writing projects, Shauna netted for herself, among other benefits, the admiration of her extended family, her friends, and her publisher; an exciting, adventure-filled week-to-week reality; and a good paycheck.

   As you look at the yes on the line above, think about the things you've gained as a result of it. Jot down as many benefits as you can.

2. The benefits of our yeses represent only one side of the equation, for even the most wonderful opportunities always demand something in exchange. There is a cost attached to every yes, be it emotional,

physical, financial, relational, spiritual, practical, or some combination thereof. Glance back at the yes you noted on the previous page.
What has that yes cost you so far? What does it continue to cost you
today? Log your thoughts below.

3. Looking at your answers to the two previous questions, and based
   not merely on the sheer quantity of them (how many entries there
   are), but also on the quality (how consequential each entry is), how
   would you assess this particular yes? Check one of the boxes below.

   ☐ In my gut, I'd say that the benefits of this yes outweigh the
     costs.

   ☐ I have a sinking feeling that the costs of this yes outweigh
     the benefits.

   ☐ The benefits and the costs of this yes feel pretty equal to me.
     I could go either way.

Assessing My Yes

_____

Write a description here of the "yes" you'd like to remove.

1. Every yes provides us some set of benefits; otherwise, we would never have said yes in the first place. For example, in saying yes to lots of work-related travel, a whole host of speaking engagements, and multiple simultaneous writing projects, Shauna netted for herself, among other benefits, the admiration of her extended family, her friends, and her publisher; an exciting, adventure-filled week-to-week reality; and a good paycheck.

    As you look at the yes on the line above, think about the things you've gained as a result of it. Jot down as many benefits as you can.

2. The benefits of our yeses represent only one side of the equation, for even the most wonderful opportunities always demand something in exchange. There is a cost attached to every yes, be it emotional,

physical, financial, relational, spiritual, practical, or some combination thereof. Glance back at the yes you noted on the previous page. What has that yes cost you so far? What does it continue to cost you today? Log your thoughts below.

3. Looking at your answers to the two previous questions, and based not merely on the sheer quantity of them (how many entries there are), but also on the quality (how consequential each entry is), how would you assess this particular yes? Check one of the boxes below.

   ☐ In my gut, I'd say that the benefits of this yes outweigh the costs.

   ☐ I have a sinking feeling that the costs of this yes outweigh the benefits.

   ☐ The benefits and the costs of this yes feel pretty equal to me. I could go either way.

Notes

Unflashy, Unspectacular, Good

―⌒―

*I look up at your macro-skies, dark and enormous, your
handmade sky-jewelry, moon and stars mounted in their
settings. Then I look at my micro-self and wonder, Why do
you bother with us? Why take a second look our way?*

―Psalm 8:3–4

THIS SESSION

*Have a group member read the following paragraphs aloud as a way to
center everyone's thoughts on this session's topic.*

It takes great courage to rightly assess the decisions we're making, the
yeses and nos paving the path on which we walk, but it's nothing compared with the courage it takes to bring those assessments before God. To
engage with the Almighty, the Creator, the Righteous and Holy One is to

have all our fabrications and facades fall away. He designed us. He built us. He knows our every thought.[3] What are we going to do, try to hide our truth from him? He knows it—fully—even before we say a word.

And so, this coming-before-God: the reason it takes such courage is not that we'll be telling God something he doesn't already know about us; rather, it's that God may choose to confirm in us the very thing we hoped wasn't true. That we're too busy for our own good, perhaps. Or that as it relates to those living under our same roof, we have somehow lost the plot. Or that over time we've developed patterns that are not serving us well. Wherever there is room for spiritual growth and maturity, God will lead us to that exact spot. And then gently, lovingly, with all the patience of a doting dad, he will say, "That. Right there. Are you interested in getting that fixed?"

In this session, you will be encouraged to bring before God all of your observations, assessments, and questions about what to keep and what to shed, as it relates to your current endeavors, obligations, and pursuits—and to do so boldly, courageously, and with open hands and an open heart.

"Part of being an adult is taking responsibility for resting your body and your soul. And part of being an adult is learning to meet your own needs, because when it comes down to it, with a few exceptions, no one else is going to do it for you." —*Shauna*

---

3. For more along these lines, see Psalm 139.

FIRST THOUGHTS

Take a few minutes for your group members to share responses to the following question:

Describe an aspect of your life where you are highly disciplined. Is it in your approach to exercise? To managing money? To coffee-drinking? To sleep? How did the system or structure evolve, what originally motivated your orderliness in that area, and what benefits do you realize from it even now?

VIDEO NOTES

Play the video segment for session 4 and use the prompts below to log your thoughts and notes.

Soul work not remedied by quick fixes

The shame we project onto Scripture

The importance of silence

Centering through prayer

Rest as healing agent

Lectio divina, or "slow-chewing" a verse

Spiritual direction: training wheels for prayer

"The only way through the emptiness is stillness: staring at that deep wound unflinchingly. You can't outrun anything. I've tried. All you can do is show up in the stillness." —*Shauna*

INVITING OTHERS IN

Discuss as many of the following questions as time and group interest permit.

1. What firsthand experience, if any, have you had in practicing "spiritual disciplines," such as the ones Shauna described in this session's video segment? If the concept is familiar to you, describe for your group an occasion when you were aided by it. If unfamiliar, describe a time when you would have been helped by such a practice, if only you'd known about it.

2. The five disciplines that have most helped Shauna during this four-year period of remaking her life from the inside-out appear below, along with a brief definition of each. Which of the five feel(s) most relevant or personally compelling to you during this season of your life, and why? Check any boxes that apply, and explain your thoughts to your group.

   ☐ Silence/solitude [The state of being contentedly alone]

   ☐ Contemplative/centering prayer [Focusing intently on and silently celebrating a singular attribute of God's, such as his graciousness, holiness, or all-sufficiency, while in a mind-set and heart posture of prayer]

   ☐ Rest/Sabbath [Ceasing from all labors for a day, according to God's original commandment]

   ☐ *Lectio divina* [Literally "divine reading"; the practice of reading and meditating on a passage of Scripture in order to deepen one's intimacy with God and enrich one's knowledge of his Word]

   ☐ Spiritual direction/counseling [Communicating with another person (or people), as a means for furthering one's spiritual growth]

> "Spiritual disciplines became a new rhythm that grounded me to a new way of believing—about God, and about myself." —*Shauna*

3. Read 2 Corinthians 7:1. What fears, obligations, obstacles, or other constraints present in your life today threaten to keep you from making "a clean break with everything that defiles or distracts" you, as the verse suggests?

4. As it relates to determining whether your current yeses and nos are honoring to God and helpful to you, how might the practice of the discipline you noted in question 2 lend greater clarity and insight to your assessment?

5. Broadening your view a bit, how might the fervent practice of spiritual disciplines help you pinpoint and prize the "one thing God is asking you to do," as Shauna referenced in the closing video segment? Have a group member read aloud the expanded passage from the book of Job (on the next page) before the group shares their thoughts.

He [God] lets loose his lightnings from horizon to horizon,

    lighting up the earth from pole to pole.

In their wake, the thunder echoes his voice,

    powerful and majestic.

He lets out all the stops, he holds nothing back.

    No one can mistake that voice—

His word thundering so wondrously,

    his mighty acts staggering our understanding.

He orders the snow, 'Blanket the earth!'

    and the rain, 'Soak the whole countryside!'

No one can escape the weather—it's there.

    And no one can escape from God.

Wild animals take shelter,

    crawling into their dens,

When blizzards roar out of the north

    and freezing rain crusts the land.

It's God's breath that forms the ice,

    it's God's breath that turns lakes and rivers solid.

And yes, it's God who fills clouds with rainwater

    and hurls lightning from them every which way.

He puts them through their paces—first this way, then that—

    commands them to do what he says all over the world.

Whether for discipline or grace or extravagant love,

    he makes sure they make their mark.

—Job 37:2–13

PRACTICING PRESENCE

Have a group member read aloud the liturgy below, and then take turns responding to the question that follows.

"Blanket the earth," you tell the snow.

"Soak the countryside," you instruct the rain.

And, "Make your mark," you tell me, you tell us all.

Not a self-made mark, mind you,

But a God-made one.

The God who thunders wondrously,

Who acts so mightily that our minds are blown,

This God is the one who wants to work in us, through us, around us,

Leaving our mark—leaving his mark—on this world.

What mark does God hope to leave on the world through you—and through us all?

"I had a set of narratives I'd been collecting for a long time—'You're not good enough.' 'You're not thin enough.' 'You're not smart enough.' 'You're not devout enough.' I was shocked to discover they didn't reflect how God felt toward me at all." —*Shauna*

4

Unflashy, Unspectacular, Good

SOLO WORK

~

Work through this section on your own, before you gather with your group for session 5.

For all the energized thrills of undisciplined living—the adventures! the risk-taking! the spontaneity! the rush!—progress *always* has discipline to thank. Take weight regulation, for instance. Both those who are overweight and those who are underweight don't take off or put on pounds without disciplining themselves when it comes to exercise and food. Or what about repairing a fractured friendship? The parties involved have to *work* at getting together, at having the tough conversations, at staying the course until they find themselves breathing fresh relational air.

It's true for financial progress—disciplined budgeting, disciplined spending, a disciplined accounting for dollars once the transactions have been made.

It's true for psychological progress. Counselors bill by the hour, not the nanosecond; growth here doesn't rush to unfold.

It's true for rehabilitative progress. Ask any stroke sufferer whether deficits were regained by just sitting around watching reality TV, and they'll laugh knowingly as they shake their heads.

It's true for the progress that comes with mastering a new hobby or skill—disciplined planning, disciplined practice, disciplined shoring up of weak spots and gaps.

And it's true for spiritual progress too. Gains never get made by coasting. We grow toward God only when we move toward him, one microscopic step at a time.

In session 4's Solo Work, we will explore five spiritual disciplines that catalyze those critical baby steps—one brave stride at a time.

"You cannot be a mystic when you're hustling all the time. You can't be a poet when you start to speak in certainties. You can't stay tender and connected when you hurl yourself through life like being shot out of a cannon, your very speed a weapon you wield to keep yourself safe." —*Shauna*

REVIEW

After suffering many years of failing relationships, failing health, and far too much static on the line between her and God, Shauna came to the realization that at the root of her problem was a little thing called *speed*. She had been moving too fast, in too many directions, on behalf of too many people besides herself, for far too long. All that freneticism eventually caught up with her.

You spent part of the last session assessing your yeses, the agreements to do and be something or someone, which may or may not be serving you well. Review your work on pages 72–74, 81–90, and then answer the following questions.

If you were to net out the thoughts you logged on these assessments, what is the common denominator of your struggle? What is at the root of the challenge you presently face? Is it speed, like it was for Shauna? Is it perfectionism or greed? Is it an insatiable appetite for more, more, more? A sky-high risk tolerance? The thrill of pleasing others? Something else? Give it some thought. Then, craft a few words of description in the space below.

Next, envision yourself bringing this root issue before God. What questions would you hope for him to answer, related to this theme in your life? Fill in as many blanks below as you wish; a sample set has been provided, to help orient your thoughts.

Example:

- *When did I first start barreling through life, demanding busyness, demanding speed?*
- *What has my need for speed cost me along the way—not just the casualties I can empirically measure but the things only you see and know?*
- *How do I get better, God? How do I slow down, look up, and grow?*

My Questions for God

_____

_____

_____

_____

_____

RECEIVE

Now comes the fun part, the part involving actually coming before Almighty God. In this section, you will be invited to experience each of the five spiritual disciplines referenced in the video segment—solitude, centering prayer, Sabbath keeping, *lectio divina*, and spiritual direction or guidance. Take your time with these divine encounters; no need to rush through them all at once. Consider setting aside fifteen or twenty minutes for each discipline. First up: solitude.

"What I'm learning, essentially, is to stand where I am, plain and sometimes tired. Unflashy, profoundly unspectacular. But present and connected and grounded deeply in the love of God, which is changing everything." —*Shauna*

Solitude

If you are generally surrounded by a throng of people—family members, close friends, an office full of associates at work, fellow volunteers at church, and so forth—then carving out time to be alone can be a daunting undertaking, not to mention one that upon first glance seems highly undesirable. Unless a person is introverted by nature, why on earth would she want to be alone? What would she do all by herself? How long would she have to stay put?

Shauna faced similar fears surrounding the practice of solitude but figured centuries of Christ followers (Jesus himself included) couldn't be wrong. Stealing away to isolate oneself from others, even for small slices of time, positions us to better hear from heaven in those times when we reengage. It is for this reason that solitude is first up in our list. "When I practice silence just for a few minutes, when I practice allowing myself to be seen and loved by the God who created me from dust, I start to carry an inner stillness with me back into the noise, like a secret," Shauna wrote in *Present Over Perfect*. "There's a quiet place inside me that I bring with me, and when I start to feel the questions, the fear, the chaos, I locate that quiet, that stillness, that grounded place" (page 93).

If you are ready to locate a similar quiet stillness, then begin here:

- Select a twenty-minute slot on your calendar soon—preferably today, tonight, or first thing tomorrow morning.
- Write the word "SOLITUDE" there and protect it as you would a rare jewel.
- When it's time for your spiritual discipline encounter, simply find a quiet place, detached from people and from your phone; sit down in a comfortable position; still yourself by taking a few deep breaths; and allow yourself to sink into the quiet surroundings, coming down and calming down as each minute ticks on by.

Pay attention to how you feel as you experience those moments there on your own. Does your mind race and churn the entire time you sit there, or does it settle down once a few minutes elapse? If you'd like to record any thoughts following the interval, space has been provided for you below.

MY EXPERIENCE WITH
Solitude

Centering Prayer

Next, slot time to practice centering prayer. You might go into your time of prayer with a theme already in mind—the theme of God's presence, his attentiveness, his measured pace, for example, especially if you're one wrestling with the issue of speed. Or you might let that theme emerge as you engage in conversation with God. For Shauna, the icon of a red heart became a vital part of her centering-prayer time, even to the point that she had it tattooed on her left forearm, as she discussed in *Present Over Perfect*:

> When I pray, I picture a red heart . . . and in the silence, I am reminded of God's love, that it began before I was born, that it will continue far past the end of my life. Before the day begins—kids, coffee, toast, little socks, little shoes, deadlines and decisions—before all that, I close my eyes, and I picture that red heart, and I remind myself what is true: that God loves me with an everlasting love.
>
> When I begin the day drenched in that love—that centering awareness of my worth and connection to God—the day is different. I don't have to scramble or hustle. Fear dissipates, and what I'm left with is warmth, creativity, generosity. I can make and connect and create and tell the truth, because my worth isn't on the line every time, at every moment. Unconditional love changes everything. It is changing everything. I can rest. I can fail. I can admit need and weakness. I can exhale. It's changing everything.
>
> And so, that red heart. I wanted to carry it with me, and I wanted it on my left arm. I'm left handed, and I want that love to be the fuel. Whatever I build from here on out, whatever I make, whatever I write,

whatever I create, I want the fuel that propels it to be love—not competition, not fear, not proving. (pages 205–206)

Whatever you choose to think on—a word, an attribute, an icon, or a name (examples of each follow, for your consideration)—commit to sitting with the concept for the full twenty minutes, allowing God to prompt you toward wholeness and holiness as you converse. The tattoo part? Totally optional.

Upon completing your Centering Prayer interval, come back to this guide to log your impressions.

Meditations for Centering Prayer

WORDS RELATED TO GOD

- Peace
- Orderliness
- Contentment
- Adoration
- Enough
- Perspective
- Sanity
- Service
- Rest
- Acceptance
- Grace
- Eternity
- Rescue

ATTRIBUTES OF GOD

- Holy
- Righteous
- Unchanging
- Strong
- Present
- Loving
- Just
- Wise
- Sovereign
- Omniscient
- Faithful
- Merciful
- Good

ICONS TO REPRESENT GOD

- Heart
- Tower/fortress
- Protective wing
- Mountain
- Cross

- Long arm
- Dove
- Light
- Flames of fire

- Open hands
- Bread and wine
- King
- The Word

NAMES OF GOD

- Jehovah Jireh, "The Lord Will Provide"
- Jehovah Nissi, "The Lord Our Banner"
- Jehovah Rapha, "The Lord Who Heals"
- Jehovah Shalom, "The Lord Our Peace"
- Jehovah Tsidkenu, "The Lord Our Righteousness"

MY EXPERIENCE WITH

Centering Prayer

Sabbath Keeping

According to God's original instruction book to the Israelite people (aka, the Ten Commandments), workers were supposed to work diligently for six days a week and then cease from their labors on the seventh. To which overworkers all across the globe scoff and mutter, "Yeah, right. Wouldn't *that* be nice?" In *Present Over Perfect*, Shauna recounted one such scene:

Several years ago, I recognized within myself deep jealousy toward a friend. I picked up on it when I realized my constant refrain about her life was, "Must be nice." When she told me about her schedule, or her family, or her day, I felt a snarky, itchy feeling bubble up inside of me. *Must be nice.*

This is the thing: her life seemed lighter than mine, easier. More free, more crafted to reflect her own preferences and passions. Mine had gotten away from me. In my blind need to be seen as hyper-capable, ultra-dependable, that girl who can handle anything, I'd built a life I could no longer handle. . . .

And in my most ground-down moments, I looked over at my friend's life and I saw that she was . . . playing. *Sheesh.* Connecting. *Please.* Resting. *Come on.* Asking for help. *What a baby.*

That's how it starts, at least for me. With disdain. A lot of "sheesh"-ing. Because if I can discount her, then I don't have to grapple with my own feelings about her life compared to mine. But I've been down this road enough to know how well it can instruct me if I let it. And so I cracked down through the disdain to see what was underneath, and I wasn't surprised, at this point, to find pure envy.

I wanted to rest and play. I wanted to connect and ask for help, and sometimes be fragile and sometimes just stop entirely. I wanted to listen to my own body and spirit instead of feeling like I was on a speeding train that left the station a long time ago and wasn't stopping anytime soon. (pages 148–149)

Perhaps you can relate. Most people can. Most people know exactly how it feels to create a too-full, too-busy speed train of a life for themselves that at some point ceases being something *they* run and starts to totally run over *them*. This is, by the way, the very dynamic God was hoping to prevent for us, by reminding us that rest is our friend.

"In the same way that I didn't allow myself to be taken care of by people, I didn't know how to let myself be taken care of by God." —*Shauna*

And so, the Sabbath. A day for rest. A day for play. A gift, if we'll see it that way. A slice in an otherwise occupied week when we clear the decks, silence the noise, hush the to-do list, and exhale. No pushing. No proving. Nothing especially impressive at all. Just us. Our most beloved ones. Unhurried exchanges. And God. Sounds enticing, doesn't it? Double-dog dare you: *Give it a try.*

Clear your schedule for one day this week, and let that calendar entry stay totally blank. You may feel a little mischievous doing this, as though you're rebelling against a hard-and-fast rule. The truth of the matter? You are. But it was never God's rule to begin with, this idea that we *are* how hard we *work*. Accept God's Sabbath gift to you. Take a day and rest. Afterward, reflect on the experience in the space below, if you're so inclined. Or better yet, Sabbath keeper, *feel free to blow that part off.*

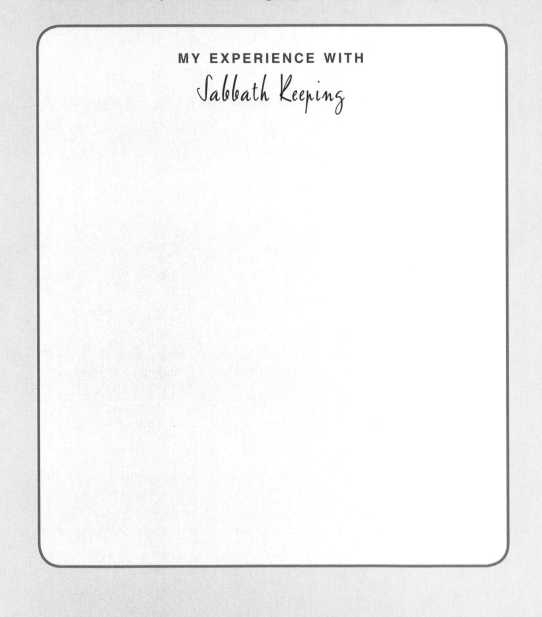

MY EXPERIENCE WITH
Sabbath Keeping

Lectio Divina

"One snowy morning recently, I felt at loose ends, disconnected from myself, from God. I'd been sick, and my mind had been anxious. I practiced *lectio divina*, selecting a passage from Psalm 8: 'When I look at your heavens, the work of your fingers, the moon and the stars, which you have set in place, what is man that you are mindful of him, and the son of man that you care for him?' As those words began to take root in me, as I read and reread them, as I prayed and listened, I felt my tangled spirit begin to untangle. I felt my breath slow and deepen. I felt a part of the natural world, governed by a good God, created with care and attentiveness. I felt my daughter-ness, my place in the family of God. And I exhaled." *—Shauna*

Now, to the practice known as *lectio divina,* or "divine reading." You'll recall from this session's video segment that Shauna had a mind-expanding experience when she was led through an exposition of the story of Peter walking on water, from Matthew 14:22–34. Upon reading the passage with fresh perspective, she realized that for most of her life, she had misinterpreted the Scriptures, projecting her own sense of shame and "less-than" status onto an exchange between Jesus and his disciple that was anything but belittling or marked by shame. She came away from that occasion wondering just how many other Bible stories she had misread over the years, well-worn tales she was sure she knew . . . but did she really know any of them at all?

Lectio divina dates back to the third century and was established as a monastic practice in the sixth century by St. Benedict (which is how the Benedictine monks got their name). The four traditional parts of the practice include reading, meditating, prayer, and contemplation, and in this interval, you're encouraged to try all four.

If you're game, then carve out your twenty-minute slot, grab your Bible and a journal and pen, and find a secluded place where you won't be interrupted. (Yes, the bathroom is a perfectly acceptable spot.) Select a passage from the alphabetized list below, organized according to common obstacles that bring us to studies such as this one in the first place, but feel free to opt for a chunk of Scripture that is meaningful to you, regardless of whether it shows up here. As always, return to this guide to log your experience, noting the passage you "chewed on," the ahas you gleaned, the divine input you received, and what you plan to do differently as a result.

Topical Passages to Chew On

Addiction: John 8:36	*Control:* Matt. 23:1–39	*Forgiveness:* Matt. 6:14–15	*Laziness:* Prov. 24:30–34	*Relationships:* 1 Cor. 13
Anger: Eph. 4:26–31	*Depression:* Phil. 4:8	*Frustration:* John 16:33	*Marriage:* 1 Cor. 7:1–40	*Scarcity:* Prov. 21:5
Anxiety: Phil. 4:6–7	*Doubt:* Gen. 17:15–21	*Gluttony:* Prov. 23:21	*Parenting:* Titus 2	*Sexual sin:* 1 Cor. 6:9–11
Arrogance: Rom. 12:16	*Exhaustion:* 2 Thes. 3:6–14	*Greed:* 1 Tim. 6:10	*Pride:* Proverbs 16:5	*Temptation:* Matt. 6:9–13
Bitterness: 1 John 2:9	*Fear:* Prov. 3:5–6	*Jealousy:* Luke 12:15	*Rebellion:* Acts 3:19	*Willfulness:* 1 Cor. 15
Busyness: Eph. 5:15–17	*Finances:* Heb. 13:5	*Joylessness:* John 15:11	*Regret:* Isa. 43:25–26	*Worry:* Matt. 6:25–34

MY EXPERIENCE WITH

Lectio Divina

Spiritual Direction

The last of the five disciplines introduced in this session is spiritual direction, or the practice of engaging with others who are on your same spiritual path, as a means of furthering your own spiritual growth. If you have never scheduled and participated in an "official" spiritual-direction session, don't get hung up on formalities here. Instead, think of this discipline simply as an intentional, spiritually oriented conversation between you and another person, aimed at uncovering and addressing a challenge that either of you is facing.

"As my friend asked me more about it, I think what might lie beneath that sort of middle missing layer of prayer is my own discomfort with need—my need. Jesus, when I think of him, is the face of such love, such deep connection, it makes me feel uncomfortable with my own need, with needs that I don't want to admit to having." —*Shauna*

To experience spiritual direction as a practice, reach out to a wise, trusted friend who knows you well and who is farther along the transformative journey than you are. Ask for an hour of his or her time, and come to the meeting armed with three to five good questions (seven samples follow). If you have never made a habit of engaging in spiritual dialogue, the first few conversations of this nature may rank somewhere between awkward and awful, but avoid the temptation to give up. Persistence pays here, God says; community is *that* important to him. Take this exhortation from 1 Thessalonians 5: "Speak encouraging words to one another. Build up hope so you'll all be together in this [the Christ-following life], no one left out, no one left behind" (v. 11).

Seven Solid Spiritually Directed Questions

If you have never broached a spiritual conversation with another Christ follower, then consider asking (and hopefully then being asked!) one or two of the questions below.

1. What important decisions are you weighing these days? How would your choices differ if you made them based on fear versus faith?
2. How would you assess your current spiritual growth? How would your [spouse/parents/closest friends/ministry partners/ etc.] assess where you are spiritually?
3. What is a single word that best describes your present emotional state? How does speaking out that word make you feel?
4. What self-care measures have you been taking lately, and how are those practices fueling you and fulfilling you?
5. How would you describe your prayer practices this [week/ month/year]? Does your vision for your prayer life match your present reality, or does a gap exist?
6. When did you last celebrate a spiritual victory of some sort? What progress had you made?
7. What is bringing you peace these days?

MY EXPERIENCE WITH

Spiritual Direction

REMAKE

The astounding and also somewhat annoying thing about spiritual disciplines is that the more you practice them, the more growth you will realize in your life. This is astounding because the guarantee is built into the system; it is annoying because the system is designed for *slow*. In other words, you can't rush through these intervals as though you're doing speed-sets at the gym. Transformation refuses to be hacked; it insists on a measured pace.

The encouragement, then, is to keep on keeping on. Keep carving out twenty-minute intervals. Keep practicing the practices you've been presented with here. Keep the conversation going between you and God, so that you can receive wisdom on how to run your life. Engaging with these disciplines isn't about adopting some rigid, unyielding ritual that is little more than yet another to-do to do. It is about relating with the One who created you, and who has staggeringly beautiful plans for your life.

"It isn't about working less or more, necessarily," Shauna wrote in *Present Over Perfect*. "This isn't about homemade or takeout, or full time or part time, or the specific ways we choose to live out our days. It's about rejecting the myth that every day is a new opportunity to prove our worth, and about the truth that our worth is inherent, given by God, not earned by our hustling. . . . It's about learning to show up and let ourselves be seen just as we are, massively imperfect and weak and wild and flawed in a thousand ways, but still worth loving. It's about realizing that what makes our lives meaningful is not what we accomplish, but how deeply and honestly we connect with the people in our lives, how wholly we give ourselves to the making of a better world, through kindness and courage" (pages 128–129).

It's about coming back to God, again and again, as often as you can, and letting the light and the life that is in him find its way in and through you.

"I don't practice these disciplines as a performance. I do them as an act of love." *—Shauna*

Notes

Living the Love

God hasn't invited us into a disorderly, unkempt life but into something holy and beautiful—as beautiful on the inside as the outside.

—1 Thessalonians 4:7

THIS SESSION

Have a group member read the following paragraphs aloud as a way to center everyone's thoughts on this session's topic.

We've made it at last—through the pain, and through the dissection of the roles that cause the pain, and through the tangle of yeses and nos that reinforce the roles that cause the pain, and through the discovery of the disciplines that guide us into a new space, a new reality, a life marked not by other people's expectations of who we are and what we should do, but rather of prizing God's opinion—and his opinion alone.

Now we've reached the fifth and final session of the series, to a session that is all about *love*.

Truly, anything whole and holy, anything healthy and strong, anything laudable and excellent has at its center a core of love. And regardless of the nuances that define the life you desire, surely it includes at least some of those descriptors—whole, not fragmented; holy, not profane; healthy, not diseased; strong instead of brittle; excellent, not tacky or cheap.

In session 5, we will explore the love that is available to you, the love that can remake you, the love that ironically has been there all along.

"The good stuff, the best stuff, the most important, richest stuff is what's happening not on the outside, but on the inside of our lives." —*Shauna*

FIRST THOUGHTS

Take a few minutes for your group members to share responses to the following question:

Describe a time when you felt deeply loved. What were the circumstances, who was involved, and why was the experience so impactful to you?

VIDEO NOTES

Play the video segment for session 5 and use the prompts below to log your thoughts and notes.

The invitation to something holy and beautiful

When the soul feels its worth

The perils of neglecting soul care

What we've been hunting for has been here all along

Remaking one's life from the inside out

"More this"

The beauty of not busy

"Is it worth it?"

"I did everything I could do to prove the worth of my soul. And then I found out that it's not what I do that proves my worth. It's that I was created on purpose, for a purpose, by God." —*Shauna*

INVITING OTHERS IN

Discuss as many of the following questions as time and group interest permit.

1. Tell your group of a time when you caught a glimpse of the holy and as-beautiful-on-the-inside-as-the-outside life that 1 Thessalonians 4:7 describes. The verse makes it sound as though this type of experience is possible, not just for a moment but for a lifetime. What thoughts or emotions come to mind as you consider such a proposition?

2. Reflect on the following lines from this session's video segment: "Without a soul, we are machines. Without a soul, we are robots. We can perform duties, but we can't feel and create and express and connect." During this season of life, what does "soul care" look like for you? Does your self-assessment land you more on the end of the spectrum that considers soul care optional, or on the end where it is valued as a fundamental part of living a connected life?

3. Read Romans 12:1–2. What do you suppose is the connection between receiving sufficient soul care and experiencing a "holy and beautiful life" more consistently? How might a foundation of holiness and beauty alter the decisions you're making these days, the placement of those yeses and nos?

4. What attitudes, expectations, neuroses, habits, responsibilities, obligations, commitments, or relationships do you think you would have to upend in order to care more faithfully and purposefully for your soul? How willing would you be to upend them, if holiness and beauty were guaranteed by-products of your hard work? What, if anything, stands in your way?

5. How do you respond to Shauna's assertion that God's love—the diamond necklace we've been frantically searching for—has been here before us, around us, inside us, all along? What does the decision to embrace that love have to do with the health and wholeness of our soul?

6. For Shauna's son Henry, what he wanted more of was "this," which in the moment meant more quality family time at home, just hanging out, playing with Legos. What is the "more this" you find yourself longing for? That thing that might just right-size your life and lighten it to the point where you could comfortably carry it for once?

"I used to believe, in the deepest way, that there was something irreparably wrong with me. And love was a lie. Now I'm beginning to see that love is the truth and the darkness is a lie." —*Shauna*

PRACTICING PRESENCE

Have a group member read aloud the liturgy below, and then take turns responding to the question that follows.

"God hasn't invited us into a disorderly, unkempt life but into something holy and beautiful—as beautiful on the inside as the outside," verse 7 of 1 Thessalonians 4 reads. Then, two verses later, the apostle Paul sheds light on how we get this done:

"Regarding life together and getting along with each other," he writes,

"you don't need me to tell you what to do. You're

God-taught in these matters. Just love one another!

You're already good at it; your friends

all over the province of Macedonia are the evidence.

Keep it up; get better and better at it."

It's the goal of it all! *Just love one another.*

Get better and better at love.

We are seen in order to see.

We are loved in order to love.

We are loved with an everlasting love.

We are loved by Everlasting Love.

We are loved to invite others into Everlasting Love.

The diamond necklace we're frantic to find?

There it dangles, around our neck.

The love has been here all along.

The time is now to bring in the love.

What tends to distract you from letting your life be all about love?

"Bring in the love! There it is. There's the love. Yep, there it is." —*Shauna's son Mac*

Living the Love

SOLO WORK

⌢

Work through this section on your own, following your group's discussion of session 5.

Finally, we come to the bridge that spans that chasm: the bridge is built by love. This journey has been toward love. We don't have to crisscross the country or cave to some contrived role or indulge harmful habits even one minute more, to find some sense of our own worth; it is here, before us, inside us, where it's always been. The chasm gets bridged only by *love*. God's love. God's great love for us. It's the only way to get from here to there.

The chasm doesn't get bridged by buffers, or by striving, or by really hard work. No, this bridge is steadied by hand-holding and song-singing, by whispered encouragement and long boat rides, by slow-cooked meals and conversation that isn't rushed. This is the love. This is where the soul feels its worth, here in the hands of God.

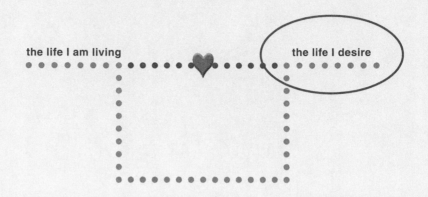

"**Through this journey of stillness, of silence, of saying no, of smaller-and-simpler, my faith became the softest place in my life, the thing I wanted to run to, when everything else felt out of control.**" —*Shauna*

REVIEW

For Shauna, the journey toward love involved not a complete rebuilding of her life but rather a return to the life she once knew. It involved reclaiming vital things she'd left behind—whimsy, yes, but also self-forgiveness, relational fortitude, deep faith. "When you begin to carry God's love and true peace deep within your actual soul, like a treasure chest, you realize that you don't have to fling yourself around the planet searching for those things outside yourself," she wrote in *Present Over Perfect*. "You only have to go back into the stillness to locate it. That treasure you've been searching for so long was there all the time" (page 93).

For you, what would such a reclamation project involve? Maybe you were totally alive in your faith in high school; or you were selfless and compassionate that summer between your junior and senior years of college, when you were serving with a missions teams. You might look back on early childhood and remember all the Scripture verses you committed to memory. Or else you could be one who was generally laid back, never pushing, never rushing, never uptight… and yet across these last ten years or so, where did that free spirit go?

On the "path" diagram below, note the dates (or general time frames) of key seasons of your life and descriptions that fit you at that time. Then, move on to the Receive section.

Reclaiming What I've Lost

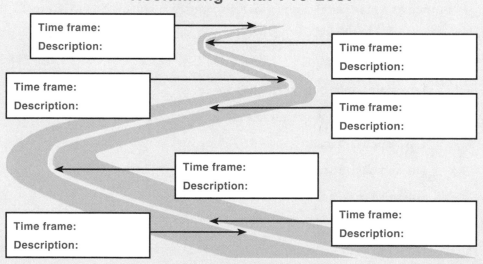

RECEIVE

Whatever it is you believe you have lost along the way—patience, perhaps, or else gentleness, an easy-going nature, resolve . . . these things can be regained the moment we surrender ourselves to love. Think of it: what problem *doesn't* love solve? For proof, read the words of the apostle Paul, keeping in mind that question: What *doesn't* love solve?

If I speak with human eloquence and angelic ecstasy but don't love, I'm nothing but the creaking of a rusty gate.

If I speak God's Word with power, revealing all his mysteries and making everything plain as day, and if I have faith that says to a mountain, "Jump," and it jumps, but I don't love, I'm nothing.

If I give everything I own to the poor and even go to the stake to be burned as a martyr, but I don't love, I've gotten nowhere. So, no matter what I say, what I believe, and what I do, I'm bankrupt without love.

Love never gives up.

Love cares more for others than for self.

Love doesn't want what it doesn't have.

Love doesn't strut,

Doesn't have a swelled head,

Doesn't force itself on others,

Isn't always "me first,"

Doesn't fly off the handle,

Doesn't keep score of the sins of others,

Doesn't revel when others grovel,

Takes pleasure in the flowering of truth,

Puts up with anything,

Trusts God always,

Always looks for the best,

Never looks back,

But keeps going to the end.

Love never dies. Inspired speech will be over some day; praying in tongues will end; understanding will reach its limit. We know only a portion of the truth, and what we say about God is always incomplete. But when the Complete arrives, our incompletes will be canceled.

When I was an infant at my mother's breast, I gurgled and cooed like any infant. When I grew up, I left those infant ways for good.

We don't yet see things clearly. We're squinting in a fog, peering through a mist. But it won't be long before the weather clears and the sun shines bright! We'll see it all then, see it all as clearly as God sees us, knowing him directly just as he knows us!

But for right now, until that completeness, we have three things to do to lead us toward that consummation: Trust steadily in God, hope unswervingly, love extravagantly. And the best of the three is love.

—*1 Corinthians 13:1–13*

Behind forgiveness, there is love. Behind selflessness, there is love. Behind optimism, there is love. Behind self-control, there is love. Behind peace, there is love. Behind humility, there is love. Behind compassion, there is love. Behind trust, there is love. Behind encouragement, there is love. Behind persistence, there is love. Behind understanding, there is love. Behind growth, there is love. Behind awareness, there is love. Behind completeness, there is love. Behind *every noble thing*, all the good things you once had but lost, there—standing tall—is love.

Bring in the love, indeed.

As you survey the text of 1 Corinthians 13, which aspect of love are you most compelled toward today? Check one of the boxes below:

☐ The patience of love   ☐ The humility of love

☐ The kindness of love   ☐ The self-control of love

☐ The forgiveness of love   ☐ The joy of love

☐ The power of love   ☐ The tolerance of love

☐ The energy of love   ☐ The trust of love

☐ The compassion of love   ☐ The optimism of love

☐ The provision of love   ☐ The completeness of love

☐ The persistence of love   ☐ The clarity of love

☐ The selflessness of love   ☐ The awareness of love

In the space below, explain why you chose the answer you did. What is it about that particular aspect of love that speaks to your current season of life?

This love—*all* of the aspects of it—is yours for the taking. God says, "This love? It's mine, for you. *All* of it—it's a gift, it is yours." This supernatural, person-specific, sure-footed love is yours. It has been here all along and asks only that you see it for what—and Who—it is.

"This is what I want to tell you: it's better here, here in the place of love." *—Shauna*

REMAKE

Perhaps the most significant strides you could take right now, as you move toward the life you most desire, are simple steps of celebration for the seemingly tiny progress you've made. During this week's video segment, Shauna encouraged us to rejoice not over every monumental accomplishment but rather over the microscopic improvements that are closing the gap between who we are today and who we most would like to be.

To that end, think back on the week that has just passed. In what ways are you practicing *presence* over *perfection*, practicing stillness over hustling and speed? Have you chosen joy despite your children's whining? Have you stayed connected to that friend over coffee despite distraction screaming at you? Have you focused on something you're grateful for instead of letting depression run roughshod over you?

Whatever the step—and however small it seemed—record it in the space below.

Based on these evidences of progress, what do you think is possible for you—and for those on each of the concentric relational circles you noted in session 3—in days to come? Dream a little, logging your thoughts in the space below.

Finally, on the next page craft a prayer to God, asking him to help you build on the success you've seen and to turn the vision you noted into a reality that honors him and satisfies you. He is with you, and he is for you. And by his power, you will prevail. Tell him what's on your heart now.

Dear God . . .

"Sink deeply into the world as it stands. Breathe in the smell of rain and the scuff of leaves as they scrape across driveways on windy nights. This is where life is, not in some imaginary, photo-shopped dreamland. Here. Now. You, just as you are. Me, just as I am. This world, just as it is. This is the good stuff. This is the best stuff there is. Perfect has nothing on truly, completely, wide-eyed, open-souled present." —*Shauna*

Notes

Present Over Perfect

Leaving Behind Frantic for a Simpler, More Soulful Way of Living

Shauna Niequist

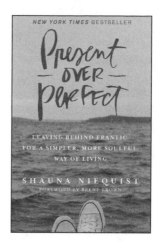

"A few years ago, I found myself exhausted and isolated, my soul and body sick. I was tired of being tired, burned out on busy. And, it seemed almost everyone I talked with was in the same boat: longing for connection, meaning, depth, but settling for busy.

"I am a wife, mother, daughter, sister, friend, neighbor, writer, and I know all too well that settling feeling. But over the course of the last few years, I've learned a way to live, marked by grace, love, rest, and play. And it's changing everything.

"Present Over Perfect is an invitation to this journey that changed my life. I'll walk this path with you, a path away from frantic pushing and proving, and toward your essential self, the one you were created to be before you began proving and earning for your worth."

Written in Shauna's warm and vulnerable style, this collection of essays focuses on the most important transformation in her life, and maybe yours too: leaving behind busyness and frantic living and rediscovering the person you were made to be. *Present Over Perfect* is a hand reaching out, pulling you free from the constant pressure to perform faster, push harder, and produce more, all while maintaining an exhausting image of perfection.

Shauna offers an honest account of what led her to begin this journey, and a compelling vision for an entirely new way to live: soaked in grace, rest, silence, simplicity, prayer, and connection with the people that matter most to us.

In these pages, you'll be invited to consider the landscape of your own life, and what it might look like to leave behind the pressure to be perfect and begin the life-changing practice of simply being present, in the middle of the mess and the ordinariness of life.

Cold Tangerines
Celebrating the Extraordinary Nature of Everyday Life

Shauna Niequist

Cold Tangerines—now available in softcover— is a collection of stories that celebrate the extraordinary moments hidden in your everyday life. It is about God, and about life, and about the thousands of daily ways in which an awareness of God changes and infuses everything. It is about spiritual life, and about all the things that are called nonspiritual life that might be spiritual after all. It is the snapshots of a young woman making peace with herself and trying to craft a life that captures the energy and exuberance we all long for in the midst of the fear and regret and envy we all carry with us. It is both a voice of challenge and song of comfort, calling you upward to the best possible life and giving you room to breathe, to rest, to break down and break through.

Cold Tangerines offers bright and varied glimpses of hope and redemption, in and among the heartbreak and boredom and broken glass.

Bittersweet
Thoughts on Change, Grace, and Learning the Hard Way

Shauna Niequist

"The idea of *bittersweet* is changing the way I live, unraveling and re-weaving the way I understand life. Bittersweet is the idea that in all things there is both something broken and something beautiful, that there is a sliver of lightness on even the darkest of nights, a shadow of hope in every heartbreak, and that rejoicing is no less rich even when it contains a splinter of sadness.

"Bittersweet is the practice of believing that we really do need both the bitter and the sweet, and that a life of nothing but sweetness rots both your teeth and your soul. Bitter is what makes us strong, what forces us to push through, what helps us earn the lines on our faces and the calluses on our hands. Sweet is nice enough, but bittersweet is beautiful, nuanced, full of depth and complexity. Bittersweet is courageous, gutsy, earthy."

Shauna Niequist, a keen observer of life with a lyrical voice, writes with the characteristic warmth and honesty of a dear friend: always engaging, sometimes challenging, but always with a kind heart. You will find *Bittersweet* savory reading, indeed.

Bread & Wine

A Love Letter to Life Around the Table with Recipes

Shauna Niequist

This is what I want you to do: tell someone you love them, and that dinner's at six.

Bread & Wine is a collection of essays about life around the table—about family, friendships, and the meals that bring us together. It's the Bacon-Wrapped Dates and mango Chicken Curry and Blueberry Crisp. It's about the ways God teaches and nourishes us as we nourish the people around us. It's about recipes, entertaining ideas, and meals to share with friends and family, made by hand and with love.

Many of the most sacred moments in my life, the ones in which I feel God's presence most profoundly, when I feel the goodness of the world most arrestingly, take place around the table. Something extraordinary happens when we slow down, open our homes, look into one another's faces, and listen to one another's stories around the table.

This is my love letter to life around the table.

Available in stores and online!

Savor

Living Abundantly Where You Are, As You Are

Shauna Niequist

Sink deep into the everyday goodness of God and savor every moment!

In this daily devotional, Shauna Niequist becomes a friend across the pages, sharing her heart with yours, keeping you company, and inviting you into the abundant life God offers.

And there are recipes, too, because spiritual living happens not just when we read and pray, but also when we gather with family and friends over dinners and breakfasts and late-night snacks. These recipes are Shauna's staples, and each one should be enjoyed around a table with people you love.

So read and learn and pray and cook and share. Remember to savor each day, whatever it holds: work and play, coffee and kids, meals and prayers, and the good stuff and the hard stuff. Life is all about relationships, and your daily relationship with God is worth savoring in every moment.